Dr. Schulze's
OFFICIAL PUBLICATIONS
Since 1979

HEALING
COLDS & FLU
NATURALLY

"For 30 years I have been treating people who have colds and flu. I have heard it a thousand times over. People start to feel bad during the day at work, and then when they come home they feel even worse. By evening they have a fever and a sore throat, they're coughing and sneezing, and they start to ache all over. In the past they would get out the cold medicine, get into bed, call work and tell the boss they were sick and that they wouldn't be coming back to work... indefinitely. Then they would get into bed and get ready for two or three weeks of living hell.

As my patients, these same people, instead of suffering, have now found a new way. Instead, they follow my advice, start my program of natural healing and herbal medicine immediatel⟩—
usually the⟩ are
absolutely

— Dr. Sc

D1470511

Dr. Schulze's
OFFICIAL PUBLICATIONS
Since 1979

Published by Natural Healing Publications
P.O. Box 9459, Marina del Rey, California 90295
1-877-TEACH-ME (832-2463)

Library of Congress Catalog Card Number: PENDING
Healing Colds & Flu Naturally

ISBN: 0-9671567-9-3

WARNING

This book is published under the First Amendment of the United States Constitution, which grants the right to discuss openly and freely all matters of public concern and to express viewpoints no matter how controversial or unaccepted they may be. However, medical groups and pharmaceutical companies have finally infiltrated and violated our sacred constitution. Therefore we are forced to give you the following WARNINGS:

If you are ill or have been diagnosed with any disease, please consult a medical doctor before attempting any natural healing program.

Many foods, herbs or other natural substances can occasionally have dangerous allergic reactions or side effects in some people. People have even died from allergic reactions to peanuts and strawberries.

Any one of the programs in this book could be potentially dangerous, even lethal. Especially if you are seriously ill.

Therefore, any natural method you learn about in this book may cause harm, instead of the benefit you seek. ASK YOUR DOCTOR FIRST, but remember that the vast majority of doctors have no education in natural healing methods and herbal medicine. They will probably discourage you from trying any of the programs.

Table of Contents

"*In Natural Healing, your job is simply to assist your body in doing its job!***"**

— *Dr. Schulze*

CHAPTER THREE

COLD & FLU PREVENTION PROGRAM

CHAPTER FOUR

COLD & FLU TREATMENT PROGRAM

CHAPTER FIVE

CHAPTER SIX

FOREWORD BY DR. RICHARD SCHULZE

THERE IS A CURE
FOR THE COMMON COLD

When cold and influenza season hits, it's my job to make sure you don't get sick.

The average American gets infected with numerous bacterial and viral pathogens every winter and gets 3 to 4 colds lasting between 2 and 3 weeks each. Most people believe this pain and suffering is just the way it is and is just plain unavoidable. After all, even our top medical doctors tell us there is **no cure** for the common cold.

On the contrary, the average patient who came to my clinic and followed my programs **did not** get sick every winter. **In fact, they stayed cold and flu-free for years, even decades!** They did this by creating powerful immune systems that destroyed and killed harmful microorganisms before they had a chance to dig in. And for those new patients who walked into my clinic already infected with a cold or flu, I taught them natural programs that crushed cold and flu infections within **24 to 48 hours.**

So you can imagine my horror when I heard people say that natural treatments and herbs for colds and flu don't work! When I heard people say that, I'll be honest, it pissed me off, that is, until I realized *they were right!*

Don't be surprised, they are right; because the natural cold and flu prevention programs I see in magazines, books and health food stores couldn't possibly work. At best they are wimpy and weak programs that might possibly, maybe, kind-of soothe scratchy throats and slightly ease your sniffles. If you think that impotent, invisible, homeopathic duck-liver crap (yes, the popular homeopathic cold remedy, Oscillococcinum, is made from duck livers, yuck!) or any other watered down herbal junk out there will save you when a powerful virus attacks your system, well, you are in for a BIG disappointment. Bacteria and viruses eat wimpy, *weak and watered-down* herbal junk for breakfast. You screw around with pathogenic killer micro-organisms and you can die. *So what do you do?*

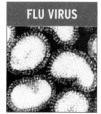

FLU VIRUS

Kill them and kill them dead!

Friends, in my clinic I learned the hard way that **this is all-out WAR!** Yes, I had to watch a few of my patients die before I figured out that I had to **turn the intensity and volume way up** with my healing programs and herbal dosages, especially when it came to treating colds and influenza. When it comes to bacterial and viral infections, you have to kick their ass before they kick yours. There is no time to waste. These are bacterial and viral *terrorists*, their bodies are wrapped in TNT and their car trunks are packed with C4 explosives, and they are driving right at you... a hundred miles per hour, and they want you DEAD. If you waste time, wimp out, or hesitate... you die.

In my clinic I used two programs. The first, well, **prevention** isn't a strong enough word for what I am going to show you inside this book. The second, my **treatment** program, is in case you already have a cold or flu. It's an all-out natural and herbal *blitzkrieg* against the invaders. Doses of Echinacea and Garlic so high even the toughest herbalists faint, and hydrotherapy and diaphoretic routines so powerful they could drive the devil itself out of your body.

What's the bottom line? Somebody is going to suffer and die... and with my programs, *I make damn sure it's the flu and not you.*

Dr. Richard Schulze

CHAPTER ONE
HORRIFYING
COLD & INFLUENZA FACTS

- **EVERY Year In America, Influenza Reaches EPIDEMIC Proportions!**

Americans get over 1 BILLION colds and flu annually.

- The average American **gets 3 colds** during the 6 winter months.

- That's over **3,800,000 new colds EVERY DAY** in the winter.

- Collectively, sick Americans will spend **over 200 million days in bed** this year.

- And collectively **lose almost 100 million days of work.**

- That's **over 10 billion dollars in lost wages** and billions more spent on drugs, doctors and hospitals!

- It costs on average **OVER $375.00 just to walk in a hospital emergency room** - that's without ANY treatment!

- If you have pneumonia, it will cost you about **$15,000.00!**

Many medical experts have been WARNING that we are overdue for the BIG ONE, a PANDEMIC (worse than an epidemic) where over 1 MILLION Americans may be dead in a few months.
— Dr. Schulze

What is Influenza?

Influenza, which is often referred to as "the flu," is an infection of the respiratory tract caused by the many different influenza viruses. These viruses can only live inside of our body's cells, eating them for food. This is why sometimes they are referred to as intracellular parasites.

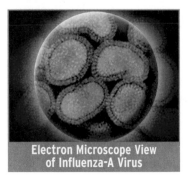

Electron Microscope View of Influenza-A Virus

When will it strike?

The general influenza season is from October through March. Many people believe influenza is worse in January, but we actually see the first outbreaks in late September and early October with **the vast majority of influenza outbreaks and deaths in October, November, December and January,** peaking the last two weeks of December and the first two weeks of January.

Influenza viral infection is usually more severe than the common cold and can include high fevers (101 to 103 in adults and even higher in children), chills, cough, sore throat, sneezing, runny and stuffy nose, as well as headaches, muscle aches and fatigue. The old west influenza was often referred to as "break bone fever" because your bones could hurt so bad during the fever it felt like they were broken. Most people stay sick for 1 to 2 weeks but it is not uncommon for people to take 3 weeks to a month to recover.

You can get viral influenza more than once a year and many people get it every year. This is because, like bacteria, viruses change and mutate. These changes are often referred to as "drifting" and "shifting." When a virus mutates gradually, this is referred to as a "drift." This constant changing enables the virus to evade your immune system's defenses and not be recognized, and infect you. When a virus changes quickly, this is called a "shift." This is an abrupt change where the virus mutates very quickly into a new sub-type. Because of this "drifting" and "shifting" it is possible for you to get the flu every year, even 2 or 3 times in one year.

How bad can it be?

If it is a **bad outbreak,** like what we have every 3 to 5 years, almost every American will get sick, 50,000 will die and 250,000 will be hospitalized. If it is a **really bad outbreak**, like the ones many medical doctors say we are overdue for, that hit every decade, like the "Asian Flu" in 1957 that killed 70,000 Americans or the Hong Kong Flu in 1968, between 100,000 and 200,000 Americans will die and another 1/2 million will be hospitalized. If it is a once-in-a-century one, like the Spanish Flu that hit about 80 years ago, **which killed over 500,000 Americans and 50 MILLION worldwide,** then we better get the shovels out and start digging because it is estimated that **over 2 million Americans will die, hospitals will be overloaded, and the sick will be dropping dead in the streets.**

What about antibiotics?

According to the A.M.A. and most medical experts, antibiotics are absolutely USELESS for colds, influenza and upper respiratory tract infections. They have no preventative nor curing effect on influenza even though American medical doctors this year will write millions and millions of prescriptions for them to their patients with the flu.

According to Fred Rubin M.D., associate clinical professor of medicine at the University of Pittsburgh and contributor to the Merck Manual – Home Edition, *"Not only are antibiotics powerless against the viruses that cause colds and flu, but misuse of antibiotics can actually do more harm than good."* According to the Journal of the American Medical Association, the high rates of antibiotic prescribing and misuse has caused alarming increases in new harmful drug-resistant organisms. In other words, **DON'T TAKE ANTIBIOTICS!**

OK, I won't take antibiotics, but what about a flu shot?

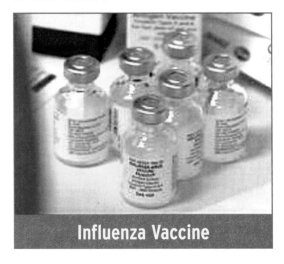

Influenza Vaccine

Every year pharmaceutical companies are making about 100 million or more doses of the flu shot. This is big business. Do the math. We're talking BILLIONS and BILLIONS of dollars. Although some doctors and patients who can't get the vaccine might turn to general anti-viral drugs, the Center for Disease Control warns that this is an untested and expensive strategy and could result in large numbers of people getting ill. There are hundreds of known influenza viruses, over 200 common ones. They never come alone and each year sees a mixture of many old viruses along with some new mutated ones.

- In 2002, the flu shot was a blend of A/Moscow/10/99 (H3N2), the B/Victoria/504/2000, the A/New Caledonia/20/99 (H1N1), the A/Panama/2007/99 (H3N2), B/Johannesburg/05/99, B/Guangdong/120/2000, and the B/Sichuan/379/99.

- In 2003, the toxic chemical blend flu shot included A/New Caledonia/20/99-like (H1N1), A/Moscow/10/99-like (H3N2), and B/Hong Kong/330/2001-like viruses. For the A/Moscow/10/99-like (H3N2) virus, U.S. manufacturers used the antigenically equivalent A/Panama/2007/99 (H3N2) virus, and for the B/Hong Kong/330/2001-like virus, they used either B/Hong Kong/330/2001 or the antigenically equivalent virus B/Hong Kong/1434/2002. These viruses were used because of their growth properties and because they are representative of circulating A (H3N2) and B viruses.

- In 2004, the toxic chemical cocktail included A/Moscow/10/99 (H3N2-like), A/New Caledonia/20/99 (H1N1-like), and B/Hong Kong/330/2001-like antigens (for the A/Moscow/10/99 [H3N2]-like antigen, manufacturers will used the antigenically equivalent A/Panama/2007/99 [H3N2] virus, and for the B/Hong Kong/330/2001-like antigen, manufacturers used either BHong Kong/330/2001 or the antigenically equivalent B/Hong Kong/1434/2002.)

- In 2005, the toxic flu shot is a blend of A/New Caledonia/20/99-like (H1N1), A/California/7/2004-like (H3N2) or the antigenically equivalent A/New York/55/2004, and the B/Shanghai/361/2002-like viruses (or the antigenically equivalent B/Jilin/20/2003 or B/Jiangsu/10/2003 viruses).

Medical doctors literally guess at which viruses they think might come around this year because the vaccines have to be prepared up to a year in advance. Even if they were exactly right with their guess as to which virus blend to put in the shot, and even got the right proportions, that still doesn't account for the new kids on the block! Influenza vaccine history shows that often, even if they guessed right, the virus mutates during the year, rendering the "flu shot" impotent. You still get the new mutated virus.

Injecting blends of viruses into your body can also be very dangerous. I remember the swine flu vaccine. It made people sicker than the swine flu itself and left others dead. This was because influenza vaccines can cause Guillain-Barre Syndrome, the immediate inflammatory destruction of the nerve sheath which causes rapid paralysis that paralyzed many who got the swine flu vaccine. All vaccines can also cause life-threatening and lethal allergic reactions.

Echinacea Flower

The **only** safe and effective defense to influenza is having a strong offense, **a strong immune system** that can kill and make antibodies for any virus that ever existed and any new one that mutates. The key to a strong immune system is a healthy lifestyle. It also doesn't hurt to have some potent herbal tonics around – like Echinacea and Garlic – that will knock the socks off any virus.

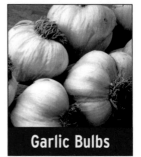

Garlic Bulbs

   Echinacea and Garlic are the 'one, two punch' for the common cold!
— *Dr. Richard Schulze*

Who is most at risk?

Up until a few years ago, "flu shots" were only recommended for those over 65 years of age, but because of the exploding viral epidemics, the shot is now suggested for anyone over 50 years old or anyone at high risk. About one hundred million Americans are considered to be at high risk. These high risk groups include anyone over 50 years old, young children, or people at any age with a chronic disease of the heart, lungs (like asthma and bronchitis), kidneys, diabetes, immune deficiency, etc. If you are not in that group, that doesn't make you immune. The Spanish Flu killed tens of thousands of healthy and strong young men 20 to 35 years of age.

More facts about viruses

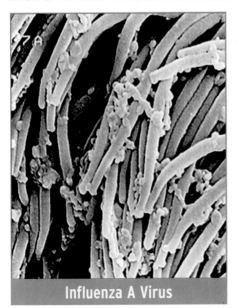

Influenza A Virus

This year the influenza virus will spread across America, and government agencies like the The World Health Organization, the Center for Disease Control and many others will collaborate and recommend what the following year's flu cocktail shot should be. After reviewing their data, **ONE HUNDRED MILLION** FLU SHOTS will be produced by 3 multi-billion dollar manufacturers.

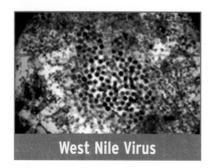

West Nile Virus

Right now I want to give you two flu vaccination statistics and thoughts that you might not get from your local medical doctor selling you or even giving you a free flu shot.

1. If you had five consecutive flu shots in any decade your chance of getting Alzheimer's Disease is **TEN TIMES HIGHER.** This is partially due to the mercury and aluminum that is in every flu shot (and most childhood shots) that builds up in the brain and causes cognitive dysfunction and disease. This is partially why the rate of Alzheimer's disease is skyrocketing.

2. *"There is no evidence that any influenza vaccine thus far developed is effective in preventing or mitigating any attack of influenza. The producers of these vaccines know that they are worthless, but they go on selling them anyway."*
Dr. J. Anthony Morris,
former Chief Vaccine Control Officer at the FDA

Poisons in the typical flu vaccine.	
Ethylene Glycol	Used as automobile anti-freeze.
Carbolic Acid	A toxic, caustic poison.
Formaldehyde	Embalming fluid that causes cancer.
Aluminum	Known to cause Alzheimer's disease, seizures and cancer.
Mercury	Found in the vaccine preservative thimerosol. Extremely toxic heavy metal that kills brain, nerve and immune cells and whose use in vaccines is linked to many childhood brain and nerve diseases.

PROBLEMS WITH VACCINATIONS?

"Several of my personal friends now have cancer, some of them have died from it. I have inquired into the probable cause of the serious increase of this horrible disease. I believe, as do many other physicians, that cancer is due to impregnating the blood with impure matter and it is obvious that the largest method by which this is done is vaccinations and revaccinations."
J.S. Preston, M.D.

"The increase in cancer has jumped four times higher in just the short time since vaccinations have been made compulsory. This terrible increase is one of the most unsatisfactory features of the Vaccination Act."
M. Hibbert, M.D.
Secretary of the Government Medical Board

"Vaccinations are how cancer is spread."
The London Hospital Gazette

"I am thoroughly convinced that the recent great increase in cancer is directly due to vaccination. I have written my report to several members of Parliament and invited them to the hospital to witness the dismal results of the Vaccination Act for themselves."
William Forbes, M.D.
Medical Director, St. Saviours Cancer Hospital
Regents Park, London, England

All of the above statements were reported and entered into the esteemed Medical Record, Volume 31, Published in New York U.S.A., January 11, 1887. THAT'S 1887!

This report was a warning to the medical profession of the United States. Great Britain had begun their Compulsory Vaccination Act and the incidence of cancer and many other diseases was skyrocketing. American medical doctors did not heed this warning, nor did the British themselves. Since then the incidence of cancer has increased **OVER 30 TIMES!**

Now, more than 100 years later...

- **In the US, from July 1990 to November 1993, the FDA counted a total of** 54,072 adverse reactions following vaccination. It also admitted that this number represented only 10% of the real total, because doctors were refusing to report vaccine injuries. In other words, adverse reactions for this period exceeded half a million.

- The FDA recently reported that **90% of doctors do not report vaccine reactions.** In the 7 years from 1990 to 1997 more than **$802 million** had been awarded for hundreds of injuries and deaths caused by mandated vaccines. Thousands of cases are still pending, but for the majority of claimants there is no money available.

MORE STARTLING FACTS ABOUT VACCINATIONS

- In 1977, **Dr. Jonas Salk** (inventor of the Salk polio vaccine) testified along with other scientists that most (87%) of the **polio cases** which have occurred in the U.S. since the early 1970's probably **were the by-product of the polio vaccine itself.**

- In the USA, the cost of a single DPT shot had risen from 11 cents in 1982 to $15.00 in 1992. The vaccine company is putting away **$12.00 per shot to cover legal costs** and damages paid to parents of the brain-damaged children who die after vaccination.

- Children die at a rate of eight times greater than average within 3 days of getting a DPT shot.

- There was never, EVER a case of autism in children before childhood vaccinations were used.

DRUGS DON'T EDUCATE YOUR IMMUNE SYSTEM.

KILLING DISEASES with harsh and dangerous chemical drugs is at best only a temporary quick fix. Your immune system is left uneducated so the same disease will return again, and usually with a vengeance the second time around. This is why people who try to KILL a cold and flu with drugs usually have constant reoccurring colds and flu. This is also why after a medical doctor cuts, burns or poisons out a person's cancer, it almost always returns. The body and immune system were never educated, no real healing took place, only part of a disease was killed and the person is still living a cold, flu or even cancer-creating lifestyle. The disease, just like Arnold in **The Terminator**, says, *"I'll be back,"* because not only do drugs only kill part of the disease, and the leftover parts become stronger and are more drug resistant, but also you didn't do anything to stop creating more disease.

CURING DISEASES with a healthy lifestyle creates a strong and educated immune system so you don't have a reoccurrence of the same problem later. Your body was supported with great nutrition and cleansing and it figured out how to HEAL you all by itself. THIS IS THE ONLY TRUE HEALING, SELF-HEALING. Diseases are the by-product of a faulty lifestyle, therefore the only real cure, the only real healing for anything, is creating a healthier lifestyle and letting your body heal you.

HEALTH and the only true healing or cure for ANYTHING, but especially the common cold, is the one your body can create by living a healthy lifestyle. Your body can heal itself of ANYTHING: all it needs it your help. Living a healthy lifestyle will also prevent future disease before it even starts by building you a strong, powerful, and protective immune system.

VIRUSES ARE KILLERS
NEVER UNDERESTIMATE THEIR LETHAL POTENTIAL

When I was only 5 years old, in 1957, I almost died from the Asian Influenza pandemic. **It was a bad one and killed over 70,000 Americans.** Many kids and older folk in my little rural town didn't make it through that winter alive. I had very high fevers and it eventually turned into bronchial pneumonia. I remember being delirious for days and, for the first time ever, seeing a worried look in my dad's eyes. A few years later he told me that I almost died that winter.

PUBLIC NOTICE

In view of the severity of the present

Epidemic of Influenza

and in order that all efforts may be concentrated on the stamping out of the disease, the local Board of Health, after consultation with Kingston Medical Society and the Mayor, has enacted that after Oct. 16th, and until further notice,

1. Theatres and Moving Picture Houses shall be closed and remain closed
2. Churches and Chapels of all denominations shall be closed and remain closed on Sundays.
3. All Schools, Public or Private, including Sunday Schools, shall close and remain closed.
4. Hospitals shall be closed to visitors.
5. No public shall be admitted to courts except those essential to the prosecution of the cases called.
6. The Board advises the public most strongly not to crowd into street cars and to avoid as much as possible any crowded train or an assembly of any kind.

Provisions have been made by the Kingston Medical Society whereby all cases applying for assistance will receive the same either by registered practitioners or by final year medical students acting under instructions. Therefore every case of illness should send in a call to a physician.

A. R. B. WILLIAMSON,
Medical Health Officer.

Public Notice during the Spanish Flu Epidemic of 1918.

I gained even more respect for viruses from my Uncle Bill. He was one of my favorite uncles, he was actually old enough to be my grandfather. See, my mother was the youngest of 16 children, so she had brothers and sisters up to 30 years older than her. Some were born before the turn of the century and her brother Bill was the oldest.

My Uncle Bill fought in both the Spanish American War with Teddy Roosevelt and also in the trenches of World War I. He was a very tough old guy, a horse soldier and definitely politically incorrect even for the 1950's. I remember I used to sit on his lap where he would roll a cigarette and light it with one hand, hold me with the other, and tell me endless hours of war stories, like the time his ship sank, flooding fast, and he had to escape from 7 decks below sea level to the horrors of the gas attacks and brutal hand-to-hand trench fighting he saw in France.

He had been shell-shocked so many times that his hair was white. He had little hearing left and had numerous battle scars that he used to show me. I once asked him what was the scariest of all of his experiences? I was very surprised at his answer. He told me that the German infantry often piled up dead American soldiers as a blockade to the advancing American soldiers. He said that it was a very gruesome sight, and horrible having to climb over your friends' dead bodies to reach the enemy. But he said that when he returned from war the dead bodies were piled up even higher on the docks and in the streets of America from the influenza deaths. He told me that was the scariest – the invisible enemy.

Influenza
Field Hospital, 1918

My Uncle Bill was the last of a dying breed of horse soldiers, and he wasn't scared of anyone. He had been shot and hit with shrapnel so many times it didn't even slow him down, but the enemy he couldn't see, and didn't know how to fight, was the scariest one of all. I could tell by the look on his face that what he saw upon his return from war in the streets of America, the hundreds of bodies piled high and thousands dying in the street, without a shot being fired, was the scariest killer he ever saw.

YOUR IMMUNE SYSTEM

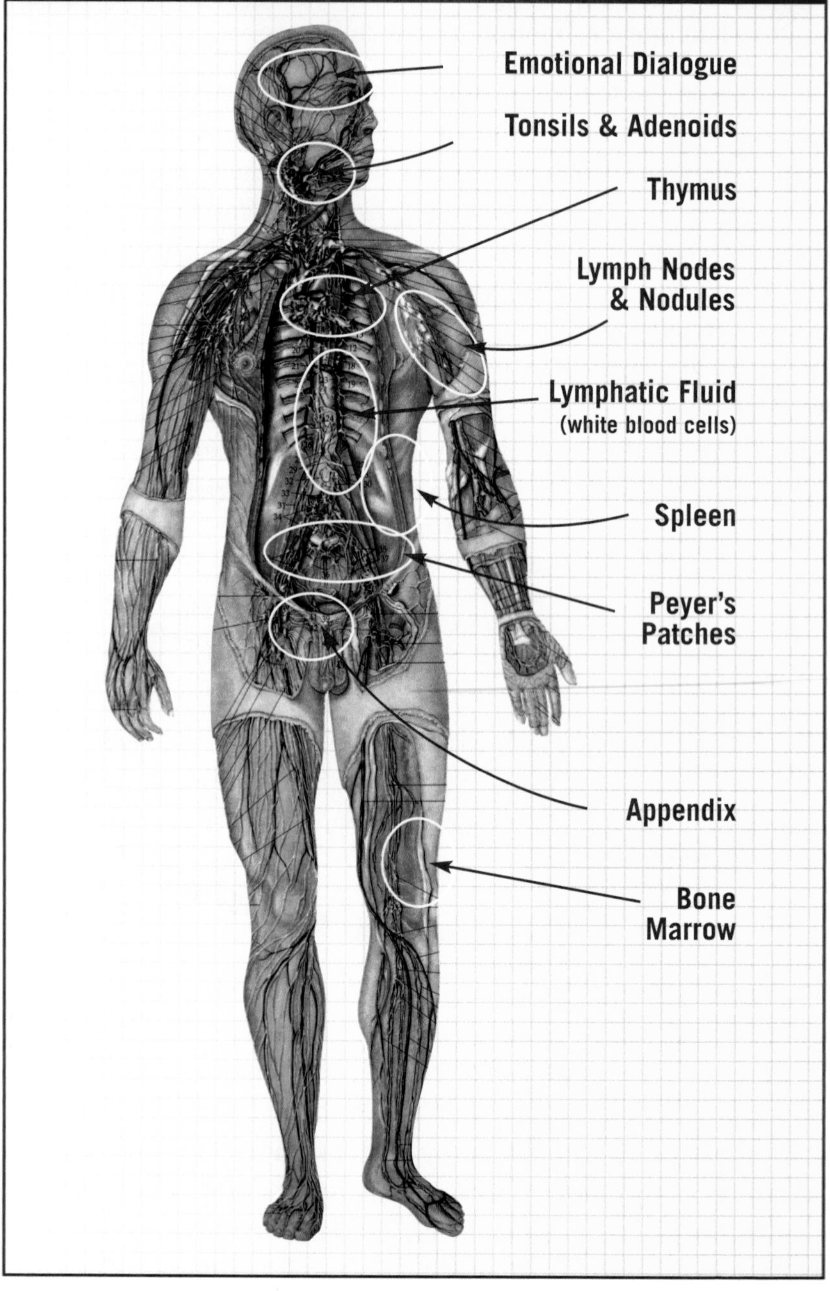

Emotional Dialogue

Tonsils & Adenoids

Thymus

Lymph Nodes
& Nodules

Lymphatic Fluid
(white blood cells)

Spleen

Peyer's
Patches

Appendix

Bone
Marrow

CHAPTER TWO
UNDERSTANDING YOUR IMMUNE SYSTEM

Your immune system is a very unique system because it is comprised of many different types of organs, tissues, cells and fluids and these various parts are located all over your body.

The Simplified Anatomy and Physiology of One of the most Complex Systems in the Human Body

Why Anatomy?

Patients and students often asked me, *"Why do you always discuss anatomy?"* The answer is quite simple. My clinical experience taught me that most people are pretty smart, have good common sense and are perfectly capable of understanding where their body parts are and what they do.

Look, medical doctors have a hard sell. Their job is not easy. They have to convince you to do something that could kill you, that will be painful if not excruciating, horrifying, disfiguring and debilitating, and that will cost you tens of thousands of dollars if not your life savings. If they didn't use fear and pressure, who would do something as crazy as this? To further ensure the success of their con job they use huge words often from foreign or dead languages like Greek and Latin and rarely explain things in a way that the average person could understand them. Often a person's biggest mistake is to not realize that medical doctors, drugs and hospitals are a big, profit-oriented business (actually the biggest money-making business in the United States). I am not saying that every medical doctor is a con-man, but the system they work for is definitely crooked and designed to try and get your entire nest egg before you die.

On the other hand, my life's crusade started when medical doctors killed both of my parents and then almost killed me as a teenager. I literally saved my life by taking my health care into my own hands. So my natural healing crusade is to teach people how to heal themselves naturally, without doctors, drugs and hospitals. To teach people that their body can and will heal itself of ANYTHING, ANY DISEASE, if they would just be willing to create a healthy enough lifestyle. I teach people how to create such powerful health that disease literally retreats and goes away.

So back to the original question, I find that the average person, given a few hours, can easily understand plenty about where their organs are, how they work and what they do. And when a person understands this, they can then understand what their medical doctor was talking about.

More importantly, with a little knowledge of anatomy and physiology my patients could easily understand that the most sane, common sense FIRST APPROACH, before choosing medical intervention, is to adjust your lifestyle to STOP doing what causes the organ to be sick. This reduces the inflammation and immediately starts the healing process. Next we START doing some programs that clear the organ's blockage and congestion, feed it nutrition and get it cleaned out and running better. What my patients quickly discovered was that their pain and discomfort would be gone in days, if not hours. Soon their illness would be gone, too, and they would be healthy. A little knowledge is a powerful healing tool.

YOUR IMMUNE SYSTEM

The major components of your immune system are the **LYMPHATIC FLUID,** which contains the many different **IMMUNE BLOOD CELLS** (like B-cells and T-cells), a **LYMPHATIC SYSTEM,** in which the lymphatic fluid flows, that includes **VESSELS, DUCTS, NODES** and **NODULES, BONE MARROW,** where all cells and all immune cells come from, **LYMPHOID AGGREGATIONS** like the **TONSILS, ADENOIDS, PEYER'S PATCHES** and the **APPENDIX** that are the immune system's communication organs and may be where the B-cells are educated, the **THYMUS,** which is where the T-cells are educated, and the **SPLEEN,** which is not only a blood storage tank but is loaded with immune cells, like a meeting hall where they can all talk and communicate with each other.

This system has one main objective, to protect you from harmful alien invaders or self-mutation. These invaders are often referred to as antigens (anti-creation or life) or pathogens (disease-creation). These harmful micro-organisms include bacteria, viruses, fungi, pollen, cancer cells, etc. Your self-mutating cells can be anything from old worn-out and dead red blood cells to cancer. Any substance that is not you, not self, or worn-out parts of you is dealt with by your immune system. It is killed and/or eaten and disposed of. It's that simple.

Your immune system has two major jobs, surveillance and action. It constantly checks your blood and body for any invaders, and if it detects any it goes into action. The surveillance is achieved by the constant checking of your digestive tract, lungs, blood, virtually every cell of your body. Almost all parts of your immune system have the ability to **survey** and **kill.**

    ❝ *Responsibility is the Foundation of Natural Healing.* **❞**
    – Dr. Schulze

The action it takes to destroy, neutralize and eliminate invading micro-organisms is fascinating and complex, and science is far from knowing it all.

I literally spent years studying this system only to discover that many authors and their books disagree on how it works, and even if they agree, their explanation is so complex you would need your accountant, a Philadelphia lawyer and a NASA rocket scientist to figure out what the heck they are talking about. So basically I decided to create my own description and chart so you can better understand this amazing system.

The following is optional

On page 32 is a chart I designed that represents your blood cells and the various cells of your immune system. This is only one aspect of your immune system but it is a very important aspect of it. The anatomy and physiology of your blood and immune cells is very complicated and volumes and volumes of medical books are spent on just this subject. At the same time many of my patients were told things about their immune cells that they did not understand, so that is why I designed this chart. My idea was to simplify the subject down to one page and a few paragraphs.

As this heading states, it is not necessary to know or even understand any of the following to be well, heal your disease and illness and build a powerful immune system; but for those who want a little better idea of what is going on anatomically, read on.

Most medical scientists agree that there is one cell that all other blood cells, both **white** blood cells and **red** blood cells, are derived from. It is sometimes referred to as a **hemocytoblast** (meaning hemo = **blood** / cyto = **cell** / blast = **create** (or) blood-cell-create), or also referred to as simply the **stem cell.**

This cell is found in the **bone marrow** and develops into either a **haemopoietic stem cell** or a **lymphoid stem cell.**

The haemopoietic stem cell

As you can see in my chart (on page 32) this cell creates or turns into **all red blood cells.** It creates **megakaryocytes,** which when mixed with **thrombopoietin** turn into **blood platelets,** which are a major component of our **red blood.** It also turns into an **erythroid stem cell** that combines with **erthropoietin** to create all **etythrocytes** or **red blood cells.**

It also creates the **myeloid stem cells** that when stimulated by **colony stimulating factors** turn into some of the most prevalent and powerful white blood immune cells in your body, **monocytes** and **macrophages.** They are usually referred to as **monocytes** when they are present in your blood and **macrophages** when in your body tissue. **Macrophage** literally translates to mean **"big eater,"** and this is exactly what they do. This gluttonous white blood cell gobbles up everything from germs to cancer; it's an eating Pac-man pig and saves your life, every minute of every day.

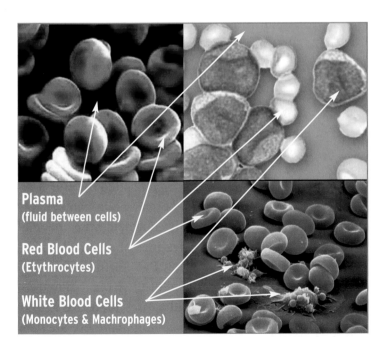

Plasma
(fluid between cells)

Red Blood Cells
(Etythrocytes)

White Blood Cells
(Monocytes & Machrophages)

This same **myeloid stem cell** can also turn into a **granulocyte stem cell** which when also mixed with a **colony stimulating factor** produces the **granulocyte immune cells** which are **basophiles, eosinophils** and **neutrophils.** These powerful immune cells are present both in your blood and in your body's tissues. These important immune cells have very specific jobs like killing bacteria, parasites and reducing inflammation.

The lymphoid stem cell

The **lymphoid stem cell** is the other main cell that the original **stem cell** creates. It is the **mother** of all of your immune **T-lymphocyte cells** and **B-lymphocyte cells.**

If the **lymphoid stem cell** is transported in your blood through your **thymus,** then it is educated there and turned into one of a wide variety of **T-cells.**

It can either become a **T-4 lymphocyte,** which is sometimes called a **T-helper cell,** a **T-8 lymphocyte,** which is sometimes called a **T-suppressor cell,** a **TK-lymphocyte,** which is sometimes called a **T-killer cell,** or a **cytotoxic cell.** Other T-cells are being discovered by scientists all the time.

The **lymphoid stem cell** can also be educated *somewhere else??* and turn into a **B-lymphocyte cell.**

Science doesn't know where this educational process takes place for the B-cell. It was originally called the B-cell because in birds —it is known that it is educated in an organ called the Bursa of Fabricius, but humans do not have that organ, so in humans it is still not understood where this B-cell is educated. Some people think it's in the **bone marrow,** the **intestines** or one of the **lymphoid aggregations** like the **Peyer's Patches, tonsils** or **appendix,** and possibly even the **spleen** or the **liver.** No one really knows. If it happens to be a lymphoid aggregation like the tonsils, adenoids or appendix, and also being that these are very popular organs for medical doctors to cut out of your body, then this could be a great explanation of why Americans have weaker and weaker immune systems and a lack of immune strength and a lack of immune cell education.

On the surface of each **B-cell** is a substance called **immunoglobulin** and the **B-cell** uses this **immunoglobulin** to create **antibodies** that are poisons, specific for various bacteria, viruses, fungi and other antigens and pathogens.

So how does this all work?

Well, first let's forget your blood platelets and red blood cells because they are your red blood and really not a part of your immune system. So how it all works is when anything like a **pathogen** (meaning disease-creating, or disease-causing) or an **antigen** (which means against life), enters your body (this can be anything like a bacteria, a fungus, pollen – anything that is not you that can harm you, or just a worn-out part of you), there is a whole complex process of your immunity that takes place.

First off the **monocytes** or the **macrophages** (remember the big eaters) attack viciously to kill and eat up any substance that isn't you. Secondly, your other immune cells from the **myeloid stem cell,** the **granulocytes,** the **basophils, eosinophils** and **neutrophils** also have their specific jobs to do in killing the invader, whether it's a parasite or bacteria. The **T- and B-cells** work differently, in a much more complex fashion.

The **T-lymphocyte cells** work together with the **B-lymphocyte cells.** First off, while the **macrophages** are off killing the invader immediately without any thought (they are just lethal killing machines), they also excrete certain immune fluids like **interleukin** and **interpheron.** Some of these fluids that a **macrophage** excretes tell your body to increase its temperature. This process of increasing the body's temperature is called **leukotaxis.** It is an amazing process to speed up the rate at which your white blood cells can move through your blood stream and your body. For every degree of temperature rise in your body, the speed at which these white blood cells can travel is doubled. This means that if you have a temperature of 104 degrees, your white blood cells can go 64 times faster than normal to get to the bad guys and kill them or eat them.

This proves without a doubt that the age-old process of reducing fevers with drugs goes DIRECTLY AGAINST what your body is doing and INHIBITS AND REDUCES THE ABILITY OF YOUR IMMUNE SYSTEM to heal you.

Other chemicals that the **macrophages** excrete tell the **T- and B-cells** where and what the deadly invader is. So the **macrophages** are not only the first cell to get to the invader, kill it and eat it, but they also excrete fluids to help your immune system work faster and also excrete fluid to give information to your **T- and B-cells.**

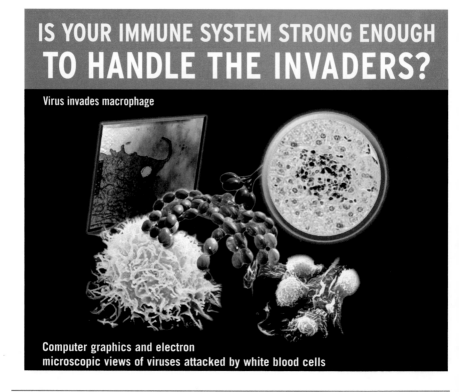

IS YOUR IMMUNE SYSTEM STRONG ENOUGH
TO HANDLE THE INVADERS?

Virus invades macrophage

Computer graphics and electron
microscopic views of viruses attacked by white blood cells

The **T-killer** cell goes out immediately and kills along with the **macrophages.** It kills quick and fast any invader that can hurt you. The **T-4 lymphocytes,** or **T-helper cells,** are the communicators. They go out and communicate with the **T-lymphocytes,** see what's happening and then communicate back to the **B-cells** what the specific invader is. The **B-cells** can then, with their surface **immunoglobulin,** create a poison that is specifically for and specifically lethal to the invader. So the **T-helper** cells are great communicators. That's why you see a little heart between that cell and the **B-cell** on my diagram. The **T-suppressor cells,** the **T-8 lymphocytes,** are also very important because it's their job to detect when the war has been won and to de-escalate the war and to stop the attack and communicate to the other **T-cells** and **B-cells** that your immune system has won. There are many other **T-cells** and their action is currently being investigated.

The **B-cells,** the other major type of cell created from your **lymphoid stem cell,** as I mentioned earlier, have a chemical on their surface called **immunoglobulin.** There are five known types of **immunoglobulin.** They use this immunoglobulin to create what is called an **antibody,** which is a specific poison that will kill a specific invader. **Antibodies** are manufactured by the B-cells with a particular shape designed to fit exactly onto the foreign invader like a key fits a specific lock. The antibody, once attached, destroys the invader.

If you are interested, re-read this section and when doing so look at the following chart I made. If you do this a few times it will all begin to make some sense to you. If it does, you might understand some of the information you hear from either your doctor or the news about disease and immunity.

If it doesn't, just skip it. You don't need to know this to heal yourself and be well.

The Basic Cellular Machinery

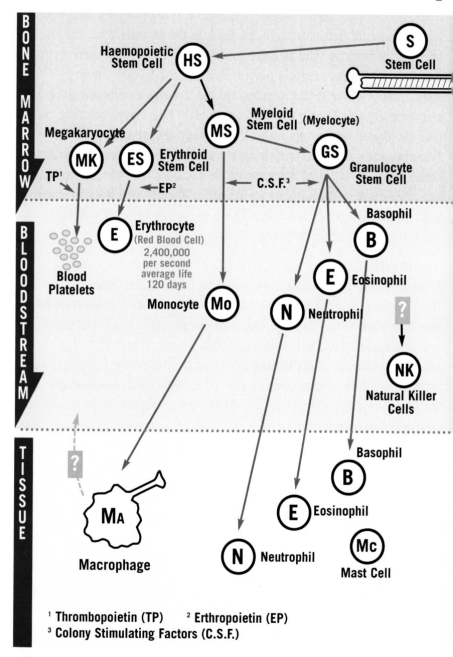

BONE MARROW

Haemopoietic Stem Cell — **HS**

S — Stem Cell

Megakaryocyte — **MK**

Myeloid Stem Cell (Myelocyte) — **MS**

ES — Erythroid Stem Cell

GS — Granulocyte Stem Cell

TP[1]

EP[2]

C.S.F.[3]

BLOODSTREAM

E — Erythrocyte (Red Blood Cell) 2,400,000 per second average life 120 days

Basophil — **B**

E — Eosinophil

Blood Platelets

Monocyte — **Mo**

N — Neutrophil

?

NK — Natural Killer Cells

TISSUE

?

MA — Macrophage

N — Neutrophil

E — Eosinophil

Basophil — **B**

Mc — Mast Cell

[1] Thrombopoietin (TP)   [2] Erthropoietin (EP)
[3] Colony Stimulating Factors (C.S.F.)

of the Human Immune System

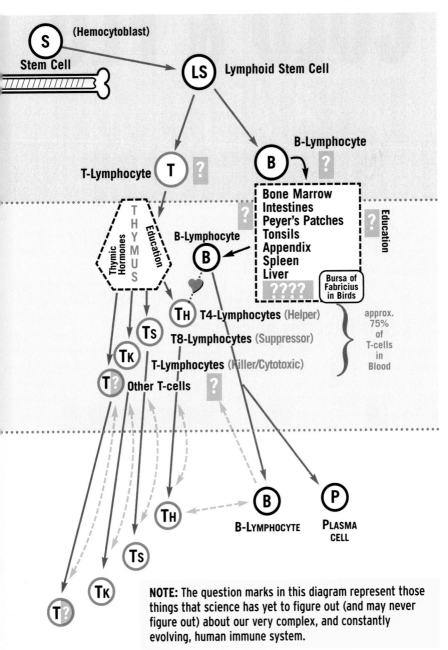

NOTE: The question marks in this diagram represent those things that science has yet to figure out (and may never figure out) about our very complex, and constantly evolving, human immune system.

Dr. Schulze's
COLD & FLU
PREVENTION PROGRAM

✔ **Start this program to stay healthy all winter long!**

✔ **Supercharge your immune system!**

✔ **Kill germs on contact!**

CHAPTER THREE
DR. SCHULZE'S COLD & FLU
PREVENTION PROGRAM

Prevention is simply the program to do before you have any signs of a cold or flu. This would be the programs to be done at the beginning of every month during cold and flu season, which to be clear would be September and October all the way to March and April. And also to be done at any time you notice that the people around you are not well.

How do you protect yourself?

I've always said, *"An ounce of prevention is worth a pound of cure."* Well, this is **my** ULTIMATE Prevention Program to be done throughout the cold & flu season.

If you are sick and tired of spending weeks, if not months, this winter in pain, in bed, stuffed up, coughing and shaking with fevers and chills, then **DO SOMETHING ABOUT IT!**

In my clinic I had thousands of patients just like you who were able to completely stop getting colds and flu during winter by following my simple and easy **Cold and Influenza PREVENTION PROGRAM.** My patients who followed this program, along with maintaining a healthy lifestyle and following my other foundational health programs, rarely got sick. Most stopped getting colds and flu completely, and haven't been sick in YEARS!

❝ *The Prevention Program is the program my patients would do every month to strengthen and enhance their immune systems so they were running at their peak ability.* ❞
— *Dr. Schulze*

HOW TO DO MY NATURAL COLD & FLU
PREVENTION PROGRAM

**Come on Friends, this program is so EASY
and only takes 2 minutes a day!
I've always said, "AN OUNCE OF PREVENTION IS
WORTH A POUND OF CURE."**

SUPERFOOD ▪ ECHINACEA PLUS ▪ SUPERTONIC

STEP 1: Take your SuperFood EVERY DAY. You need powerful nutrition to build a powerful immune system.

STEP 2: Take 2 droppersful of Echinacea Plus and 2 droppersful of SuperTonic five times a day for six straight days – do this the first week of every month.

BUT, if you're like most of my patients, remembering to do something 5 times a day is difficult, if not impossible. So for you I have created the following drink. Make it first thing in the morning and sip it all day. At the end of the day you will have taken all of your herbal medicine.

Dr. Schulze's Cold & Flu
PROTECTION DRINK

- 10 droppersful of Dr. Schulze's Echinacea Plus
- 10 droppersful of Dr. Schulze's Famous SuperTonic
- 8 ounces of PURE WATER
- 8 ounces of Organic APPLE JUICE

Make my Protection Drink and sip it all day long. Drink for 6 straight days - the first week of every month all during Cold & Flu Season.

SUPERFOOD

Builds a powerful immune system!

Your body needs vitamins, minerals, amino acids, enzymes and many other nutrients to manufacture immune cells like T-cells, B-cells and macrophages, rebuild immune organs like the bone marrow and thymus, and create vital immune chemicals like interferon, interleukin and antibodies that you need to destroy any bacteria, virus, or pathogen. Some nutrients on their own, like Vitamins A and C, have natural infection-fighting and immune-stimulating ability.

When you have an infection the best way to guarantee that you have a constant rich supply of vitamins and minerals in your bloodstream at all times is to build your immunity with daily use of **SUPERFOOD.** This will also guarantee that when your body needs to build up its immune system, it has the building blocks to do the job.

I always tell people, herbs like Echinacea are the greatest at stimulating your body to make new immune cells and boosting your immune system, but what do you think you are going to build all those immune cells from? Beer, pizza, potato chips? Keeping your blood loaded with nutrition assures that you have a constant storage supply of nutrients that your body can use at any time to manufacture anything it needs. All of my herbal formulae tell your body to do something; **SUPERFOOD** gives your body the fuel it needs to do these things. It makes all of my herbal formulae work 100 times better.

Botanical Ingredients

Spirulina Blue-Green Algae, Chlorella Algae, Alfalfa Grass, Barley Grass, Wheat Grass, Purple Dulce Seaweed, Beet Root, Spinach Leaf, Rose Hips, Orange and Lemon Peels and NON-Active Saccharomyces Cerevisiae Nutritional Yeast.

SuperFood Dosage

In a blender mix 8 ounces of organic fresh fruit juice, 8 ounces of pure water, 1/2 cup of fresh organic fruit and 2 tablespoons of SUPERFOOD.

Real People. Real Results.

" *Dear Dr. Schulze,*
I have been taking your SuperFood for almost a year. I have also done your Intestinal Formula 1 & 2. I also got your Echinacea Plus and SuperTonic. Every time I felt like I was coming down with something, I would take some. I'm telling you, I would feel better RIGHT AWAY!! **"**
— D.K. Sun City West, AZ

" *Dr. Schulze,*
I usually get at least 3, if not 4, colds every winter. I don't mean little sniffles, I mean in bed for 2 weeks dying kind of things. Well two years ago I started on your Echinacea Plus, along with your SuperFood, Intestinal Formula #1 and SuperTonic and I have not had one single cold in two years. It literally is a miracle. **"**
— B.L. Cheyenne, WY

ECHINACEA PLUS

The Strongest Booster to Supercharge your Immune System.

I spent 20 years in the clinic dealing with tens of thousands of patients that all had a cold or flu at some time. I witnessed the miraculous effectiveness of Echinacea on a daily basis. In the last decade hundreds of medical and scientific articles have been written exalting Echinacea and explaining how it works.

Echinacea Plus supercharges your immune system by stimulating you to build more immune cells and immune chemicals. This protects you before any bacteria or virus invades you, or if they do, your immune system can gobble them up before you even notice any symptoms. Over the years, many of my patients who used their Echinacea Plus on a regular basis never got sick.

Echinacea contains phytochemicals such as polysaccharides, isobutyl amides, polyacetylenes, cichoric acid, echinacoside and cynarin. These chemicals are known for their many healing benefits such as hyaluronidase inhibition which protects your cells by stopping bacteria, viruses, and other disease-causing organisms from penetrating your cell wall. These chemicals also stimulate and increase the number of leukocytes (white blood cells) in your body. These cells, T-cells, B-cells, granulocytes, macrophages, etc, are some of the main components of your immune system and directly kill bacteria and viruses. Other chemicals in Echinacea increase phagocytosis, the ability of the above mentioned cells to destroy and dispose of bacteria, viruses, fungi and other disease-causing microbes. Echinacea increases production of gamma globulins. These are the chemicals that coat your B-cells and are used to make antibodies. Antibodies are chemicals that kill specific bacteria, viruses and other pathogens that can hurt you and make you sick.

There are literally hundreds of other known and researched healing and protecting abilities of Echinacea besides colds, flu, sore throats and upper respiratory infections. A partial list includes inhibiting tumor growth, killing strep and staph bacteria, halting urinary tract infections, healing infected wounds, relieving hives and allergic reactions, stopping allergies, neutralizing toxic and poisonous insect and animal bites and stings, etc.

Echinacea Plus also contains Garlic. Why do I use Garlic instead of Goldenseal root? There is really no contest. Goldenseal is a much milder antibacterial bitter herb. It is wonderful for the sensitive areas of the body. But compared to Garlic, GET REAL!

Garlic is one of the strongest medicinal plants on Earth. Unlike Echinacea, which can only be documented in Native American Indian usage from the 17th century, the medicinal use of Garlic has been documented, if not worshiped, since the beginning of recorded history. From the Egyptians and Greeks to the Romans, Garlic was used as both food and strong medicine to strengthen and heal the

Real People. Real Results.

" *Dear American Botanical Pharmacy,*
I can't begin to tell you how your SuperFood, Intestinal Formula #1 and Echinacea Plus turned my life around. I used to go to bed at 7:00pm and now I can stay up until 10:00pm! I can actually eliminate (poop) every day instead of twice a week. And most of all, I've kept myself from getting sick several times in the past few months with Echinacea Plus. I had the "flu from hell", couldn't get rid of it. Had a miserable cough, the works. I discovered the Echinacea Plus and did what Dr. Schulze said and drank a bottle and a half in three days. Bye, bye flu (and cough)! One has to experience for themselves if something works. I experienced a change in my health in a very short period of time. May you and your staff, especially the "main man" flourish and prosper always. **"**
— Love, S.B. Clearwater, FL

body. In research it has been diluted 1 part in 125,000 and still kills bacteria. In fact, just the odor has proven to be highly antibacterial. It is an extremely effective and powerful broad-spectrum antibiotic, which means it kills all types of bacteria on contact, gram-positive and gram-negative. Garlic's use as an antibacterial drug in Russia is so esteemed it has been nicknamed Russian penicillin.

Garlic has been proven to destroy many types of bacteria including streptococcus, staphylococcus, typhoid, diphtheria, cholera, E. coli, bacterial dysentery (travelers' diarrhea), tuberculosis, tetanus, rheumatic bacteria, and many others.

Garlic is also a very powerful antiviral agent proven in the laboratory. Many doctors feel it's the cure for the common cold. It destroys various viruses that cause upper respiratory infections and influenza, the ones I said at the beginning of this newsletter that antibiotics are useless against. Garlic destroys on contact the viral infections of measles, mumps, mononucleosis, chickenpox, herpes simplex #1 and #2, herpes zoster, viral hepatitis, scarlet fever, rabies and others. So while some say that the reason you don't catch colds when you eat Garlic is because no one will come near you, remember, Garlic is also a powerful antiviral agent.

So Echinacea and Garlic are the dynamic duo, "The One, Two Punch" for the common cold. Echinacea will enhance, stimulate and strengthen your immune system, to protect you, and Garlic will destroy the invader on contact.

Cayenne pepper, which is unique to my formula, increases your blood and lymph circulation, which makes this formula 10 times more effective than Echinacea by itself.

Botanical Ingredients

Fresh Echinacea angustifolia root juice, Echinacea angustifolia root, Echinacea purpurea seed, Fresh Garlic bulb juice and Habanero pepper.

Echinacea Dosage

The dosage is dependent on the situation. My suggested clinical dosages are as follows, which I might mention are double what most other armchair herbalists suggest. But these dosages created successful healings in my clinic year after year. Oddly enough the most effective dosage and treatment using Echinacea is like a treatment of antibiotics. Echinacea must be taken steadily over a period of about 2 weeks for maximum immune protection.

For preventative immune boosting, but with no current health problem:
Use 2 droppersful, about 60 drops, 5 times daily until you have consumed 2 fluid ounces or 60 milliliters. This will take about 7 days. Do this at the beginning of each month for the best cold and flu prevention.

You have that uh-oh feeling, no specific symptoms but "I think I'm coming down with something":
Use 4 droppersful, about 120 drops, 5 times daily until you have consumed 2 fluid ounces or 60 milliliters. This will take 3 to 4 days. Start immediately.

Onset of fever, chills or any of the symptoms of a cold or flu:
Use 4 droppersful, about 120 drops, 8 times daily (or every other hour you are awake) until you have consumed 2 fluid ounces or 60 milliliters. This will take about 2 days. You may continue this dosage for a week and then reduce dosage.

High fever, sore throat, yellow mucous, coughing and/or sneezing:
Use 4 droppersful, about 120 drops, every hour you are awake, about 16 times a day until you have consumed 2 fluid ounces or 60 milliliters. This will take about one day. You may do this for 2 to 3 days before you lower your dose.

NOTE: *There are no toxic side effects with Echinacea and no known overdosage. Health circle rumors abound that if you take too much Echinacea or take it for too long a period of time you could burn out your immune system. Over the years in my clinic I had many an Echinacea junkie and never saw one case of depressed immunity because of their habit. I had many patients that took Echinacea every day for 2 to 3 years without a break. All I saw was miracle healings.*

On the contrary, I saw many people stay sick and not recover because they didn't take enough herbs.

Echinacea is a strong medicinal herb. All medicinal and toning herbs are best used for a period of time and then stopped for a week or two. This is true of most medicinal herbs.

DR. SCHULZE'S PERSONAL
COLD & FLU BLASTER

To protect myself in the clinic I needed to develop routines far beyond what the normal person needs because when cold and influenza season hit, I had to take care of my patients and stay on my feet. One of the ways I stayed healthy even during the peak of cold and flu season was this herbal drink. Eventually my special and personal routines ended up being the favorites of my patients, too. One such routine was what I called my COLD AND FLU BLASTER.

I would take a small glass and put in:
- 8 droppersful of **Echinacea Plus**
- 2 droppersful (lightweight) of **SuperTonic,** 4 droppersful (medium), 6 droppersful (strong), or 8 droppersful (my kind of guy/gal)
- one ounce or two of fresh-squeezed organic apple juice.

I would gargle with this for at least 15 seconds, if not a full minute, and then swallow what was left over, if any, of the drink.

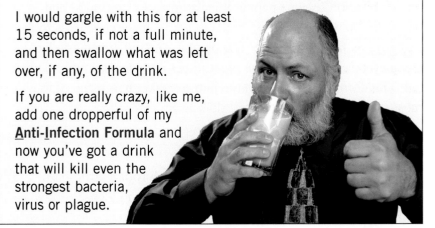

If you are really crazy, like me, add one dropperful of my **Anti-Infection Formula** and now you've got a drink that will kill even the strongest bacteria, virus or plague.

SUPERTONIC

My patients called it the cure for the common cold – It kills germs on contact!

Sometimes the invaders are so powerful they sneak by the strongest immune systems. If this happens it is important to mount an additional attack to stop the infection dead in its tracks. SuperTonic is a strong herbal plague formula that helps with all the symptoms of colds and flu and should be used in conjunction with my Echinacea Plus.

SuperTonic destroys bacteria, viruses and fungi ON CONTACT. It breaks up and relieves congestion in the sinus and lungs, promotes expectoration and helps your body manage a fever. Many of my patients swear that SuperTonic is the cure for the common cold. I believe it is too. This formula is not a replacement for any of the above formulae, but should be used in addition to them.

The FRESH JUICES of organic raw Horseradish root first and foremost drive this formula to your head, sinus, throat and lungs where you need it. The organic raw Garlic juice and its next of kin, organic raw Onion juice, are the two best virus and bacteria killers in the herbal world. The organic raw Ginger root juice and organic raw Habanero Cayenne pepper juice stimulate your blood and lymphatic flow like no other herbs to get your immune cells to the bad guys as fast as possible. The organic raw unfiltered apple cider vinegar preserves all of these plant juices and cleanses your body too. This formula is a pain in the butt to make, but is one of the most requested during cold and flu season.

Botanical Ingredients

FRESH ORGANIC JUICES of Horseradish root, Garlic bulb, Onion bulb, Ginger root and Cayenne peppers in a base of raw unfiltered apple cider vinegar.

SuperTonic Dosage

Take 1 to 4 droppersful in a shot glass. First-timers may want to mix this dosage half and half with water. Whether you dilute it or take it straight, gargle with it for a minute, and then swallow. Some of my advanced patients would take it as I do, swig it straight from the bottle and then hold on to your chair.

Real People. Real Results.

" *Dear Dr. Schulze,*

You should win the Nobel Prize because you have definitely discovered the cure for the common cold. Every winter I get four or five colds. They start with a fever, then a sore throat, then into the sinus and lungs and into bed for a week. No doctor and no medicine has ever been effective, until you, EVER. This year everybody is sick around me. I have had three colds start already this year, but what I did different is when I felt the fever and sore throat coming on, I gargled and swallowed your SuperTonic like you said to do. In each instance, miraculously, the very next day the cold was gone. Many of your formulas are a real blessing, but your SuperTonic is the best. "
— *R.F. Boston, MA*

FOUR EXTRA TIPS TO HELP
PREVENT COLDS & FLU

- **AVOID TRAVEL AND CROWDS**
  Use my **Air Detox** to kill germs and micro-organisms in the air.
- **DRINK YOUR OWN WATER**
  Take bottled or filtered water with you if you do travel or when going out.
- **WASH YOUR HANDS OFTEN**
  This is the #1 way to keep from getting infected.
  It's OK, GET OBSESSIVE!
- **AVOID UNHEALTHY PEOPLE AND TV**
  Nothing suppresses your immune system like bad attitudes and bad news.

YOU'RE SICK?

STOP YOUR COLD OR FLU NOW!

YESTERDAY you came home from work with that "UH-OH" feeling.

LAST NIGHT you got a fever and a scratchy sore throat and you went to bed hoping it would be gone this morning. But it's not.

TODAY you are much worse. You are sweating with a fever, your throat is killing you and your nose is starting to get blocked up.

SEE NEXT PAGE...

Dr. Schulze's Famous

COLD & FLU
TREATMENT
PROGRAM

✔ **Start this program at the first sign of symptoms!**

✔ **Antibiotics are useless against any viruses!**

✔ **Stop a cold or flu dead in its tracks!**

CHAPTER FOUR
DR. SCHULZE'S COLD & FLU TREATMENT PROGRAM

Remember, the people who don't get well using natural healing don't get well because they didn't do enough... not because they did too much.

At the first signs of any Cold or Flu infection, to stop it dead in its tracks, START THIS PROGRAM IMMEDIATELY! You have 2 choices, 24-48 hours or HEALING, or a few weeks of SUFFERING.

Introducing my Cold and Flu Treatment Program

Used in my CLINIC but never before released to the public until now...

When I was only 5 years old I almost died from the Asian Flu. I was lucky, it killed many kids in my town. That winter over 70,000 Americans died from influenza. The high fevers I had badly scarred my already deformed heart.

As a teenager I got very sick with many colds and flu, EVERY winter. As you have read in chapter one, Americans get over 1 Billion colds and flu every year, averaging over 3.5 colds and flu annually for every man, woman and child. Well, I got my share and somebody else's share because I got sick about every other month, and when I got sick, I got hit hard and I went down hard. Each cold or flu lasted at least 2 weeks and was pure hell with unbelievable head and body pain. A big part of me healing myself was not just healing my heart, but was figuring out a way to avoid getting horrible colds and flu every few months.

Getting healthier dramatically reduced the amount of colds and flu I got every year. Getting healthier strengthens your immune system, which generally protects you from getting sick in the first place. But I still got a few every year even though I was healthier so I needed a plan.

I studied hundreds of years worth of herbal formulae that were specifically designed for colds and flu. I researched the individual cold and flu herbs too. I also developed my plague formula (SuperTonic) while still in herbal college and I also researched natural healing and hydrotherapy routines that were supposedly effective. For a few years I experimented on myself, students and patients until I finally came up with an effective program that worked. It is a miracle.

You have read about it every year in my newsletter, and you have read about the results. Last year I put it into a kit. My new COLD & FLU PROGRAM. Next time you get a cold or flu, use it, and you will see that it is true; there actually is a cure for the common cold!

Treating Colds and Influenza begins with my new COLD & FLU PROGRAM. Period.

Antibiotics are useless even though patients demand them, and flu shots are – pure and simple – an **ineffective** gamble with YOUR health!

No one can afford to be knocked on their back for 5 days or longer. Airborne viruses do just that and infect millions of people every year.

Strengthening your body's natural ability to fight against viruses is your **FIRST STEP** in getting the upper hand against Colds and Influenza this season.

Dr. Schulze's Famous
COLD & FLU
TREATMENT PROGRAM

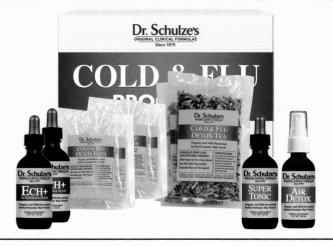

Includes:

2 **Echinacea Plus**
1 **SuperTonic**
1 **Air Detox (2 oz.)**
2 **NEW Cold and Flu Detox Teas**
2 **NEW Cold and Flu Detox Bath Packs**
1 **25 Ways to Prevent & Treat a Cold/Flu Book**
1 **Quick Start Directions Includes:**

- **How to Use the Herbs**
- **Hydrotherapy and Bath Pack Instructions**
- **Dr. Schulze's Treatment Program**
  which includes his Food Program,
  Elimination Program, Movement Program,
  Rest Program, Attitude Program and "Just
  Say NO to Drugs" Program.

HOW TO DO MY NATURAL COLD & FLU
TREATMENT PROGRAM

During the Day

During your waking hours consume 1 entire bottle of my Echinacea Plus (that is 2 fluid ounces). You will also consume 1/2 bottle (that's 1 ounce) of my SuperTonic. You should space out your doses so that you are consuming these 2 formulae throughout the day. The best way to insure your success at getting all of the herbal tonics consumed is to make 2 of my Cold & Flu Detox Drinks (see recipe at right) and make sure that you sip one, and finish it, in the first part of the day, and make a second drink and sip it and finish it during the second half of the day.

NOTE: *If this drink is too strong, you can add more juice and water as you like, but remember that you must consume 2 of these entire drinks during the day.*

Cold & Flu Detox Drink:
- 1 ounce **Echinacea Plus** (1/2 bottle)
- 1/2 ounce **SuperTonic** (1/4 bottle)
- 8 ounces of fresh, organic, Apple Juice or Citrus Juice
- 8 ounces of Distilled Water

During the Evening

In the evening for 2 Days DO this hot bath hydrotherapy routine.

This routine is diaphoretic and it will make you sweat profusely. This will help to detoxify your body. Remember, a fever is your friend as long as you stay hydrated. For every degree of temperature rise in your body, the speed at which your bacterial and viral fighting white blood cells can travel IS DOUBLED! So lets get hot and sweaty!

STEP 1: Turn the heater on in your bathroom, and get the room as hot as you possibly can, like a sauna. If you don't have a separate

CAUTION: *It is possible to feel a little faint when doing this routine. If possible you should always have a friend around when doing this routine to give you a cold slap with a washcloth or a dose of Cayenne Tincture while you are in the hot tub, if needed.*

heater in your bathroom, get a small portable heater but keep it far away from the bathtub. Always make sure that any heating appliance in your bathroom is plugged into a special ground fault electrical outlet for safety. GET THE BATHROOM VERY HOT!

STEP 2: Prepare the tea. Place the loose Cold & Flu Detox Tea into a medium sized pan with 50 ounces of cold distilled water. Stir the herbs to get them fully saturated with water. Put the pan on the stove and turn up the heat. As the mixture heats up, stir the herbs even more. When the mixture comes to a boil, turn off the heat and let it sit.

STEP 3: Fill your bathtub with hot water, about as hot as you can stand it. Then put the Cold & Flu Detox Bath Pack of herbs into the water and squeeze the bag numerous times. You will see the bath water, changing color and smell the aroma of the herbs. Spray 10 to 12 pumps of Air Detox into the air, saturate the air with this formula and continue to spray it in the air during this entire routine.

STEP 4: Now strain the Cold & Flu Detox Tea through a stainless steel sieve into a jug and take it with a tea mug into the bathroom.

STEP 5: Get into the bath and start drinking your hot tea. **You must consume all 48 ounces of it while you are in the bath.** Also while you are in the bath, keep squeezing the Cold & Flu Detox Bath Pack herbal bag to keep releasing the herb's healing plant chemicals into your bath.

STEP 6: Add more hot water into the bath. Make the bath as hot as you can stand it. Also force yourself to drink all of the tea. The bath should take 30 minutes.

When you are done, rinse off cool, dress warm and go straight to bed.

- It is normal to feel your skin tingling in this bath.
- It is even possible that you might feel strong tingling, maybe even a little burning in your most sensitive areas, this is OK.
- Also, like any herbal tea, the herbs in the bath may stain, so wear old sweat clothes.

6 ADDITIONAL HEALING STEPS

Don't get knocked on your butt again, fight back, and knock your cold and flu on ITS butt instead. Get well and get back on your feet... FAST!

Step 1: Food Program

Starve a cold and feed a fever, **or was it** feed **a cold and** starve **a fever** – what the heck did grandma say anyway? **The real answer is STARVE EVERYTHING.** Anytime you feel the first signs of anything coming on, **STOP EATING** and **FLUSH your body out** with pure water, herb tea and fresh juices. It takes a lot of energy to process, digest, assimilate and eliminate food. If you continue to eat while having a purification it is harder for your body to heal. If you stop eating, your body can utilize ALL of its energy and resources to help you get well. Juices are the concentrated liquid extract of food. This means they can be digested with very little effort and are concentrated sources of vitamins, minerals and other nutrients. Your body needs these nutrients to manufacture immune cells, rebuild immune organs, and create vital immune chemicals, like antibodies, that you need to destroy any bacteria, virus, or pathogen. Some of these nutrients on their own, like vitamins A and C, have natural infection-fighting and immune-stimulating ability. These juices also flush toxins and poisons out of the body and also naturally purge the body and open up the elimination organs. So stop eating and get the juicer out. Use local organic produce that is in season. You can dilute the juice with up to 50% water. For some this makes it easier to digest. **You must consume at least one gallon (128 ounces) of liquid each day on this program.** That can be a combination of fruit juice, vegetable juice, herb tea and pure water. **Do not forget to take your SuperFood!** And if you are sick, take it 2 times a day.

GARLIC Consume at least 3 cloves of fresh RAW garlic each day. NO deodorized capsules. **Garlic is a potent antiviral and antibacterial herb.** It destroys both gram-positive and gram-negative bacteria. In other words it's an all-natural broad spectrum antibiotic. But the best part is that, unlike chemical antibiotic pills, Garlic leaves all of your friendly and good bacteria alone and alive, the bacteria that you need to be healthy. Pharmaceutical antibiotics are non-selective in their destruction of bacteria and destroy even your good bacteria. That is why you end up with digestive problems, constipation, and yeast and fungal overgrowth infections.

Garlic, on the other hand, actually **enhances** your intestinal micro-flora and selectively kills the bad bacteria. Mother Nature does it best again!

NOTE: If you have influenza or pneumonia don't hesitate to use 10 - 50 cloves of raw Garlic a day to save your life!

❝A great healing dose is at least 3 cloves of FRESH, RAW Garlic every day. ❞
— Dr. Schulze

DR. SCHULZE'S POTASSIUM BROTH RECIPE (VEGAN "CHICKEN SOUP")

This is a great-tasting addition to your cleansing program. It will flush your system of toxins, acid and mucous while giving you concentrated amounts of minerals. It is a classic remedy for colds and flu.

1. Fill a large pot with:
   - 25% potato **peelings**
   - 25% carrot **peelings** and **whole** chopped beets
   - 25% chopped **whole** onions and Garlic
   - 25% **whole** chopped celery and dark greens.

2. Add hot peppers to taste. Add enough distilled water to just cover vegetables and simmer on very low temperature for 1-4 hours.

3. Strain and drink only the broth, put the leftover vegetables in your compost. Make enough for two days, refrigerate leftover broth. Use only organic vegetables! We do not want to consume any toxic, immune suppressive insecticides, pesticides or inorganic chemical fertilizers while we are on a detoxification program.

My broth will flush you out and build you up. Start it now!

Step 2: Elimination Program

To help your body defend itself, it is important to help it get rid of all its accumulated waste and toxins by stimulating your elimination organs. Therefore make sure that ALL of your elimination organs are working, ESPECIALLY YOUR COLON.

Cleanse your bowel daily. Immediately begin my 5-Day Bowel Detox using both Intestinal Formula #1 and Intestinal Formula #2.

Make sure your liver, gallbladder, kidneys and bladder are working freely by using either the **5-Day Liver Detox** or **5-Day Kidney Detox.** Choose which flush to do based on your personal constitution or family history of illness. You also need to sweat, which leads us to the next section.

Step 3: Movement Program

A. AIR: Fresh air is essential!

Keep at least one window open in the house no matter how cold and snowy it may be outside. Keep moving, but use your head. Take a walk outside, breathe deeply, and work up a little sweat.

B. BLOOD: Keep your blood moving with hydrotherapy!

In the morning take a hot and cold alternating morning shower always ending in cold. Start by taking a nice warm shower. Then, when you're ready, turn all the hot water off. Breathe, it won't kill you. Yell if you need to and after at least 15 seconds of pure cold, turn back up the hot to a very warm temperature. Repeat this seven times and end with cold. (Use cool, not cold, water at first if you have a bad heart.)

C. CIRCULATION: Keep your body moving!

You may modify your workout, but don't stop. Listen to what your body is telling you. Modify your exercise, modify your workouts, but don't totally stop unless you are just plain exhausted. Continuing your workouts keeps you breathing and promotes blood and lymphatic (immune system) circulation. This will speed up your immune system to fight disease and also speed up your healing process.

Step 4: Rest Program

There is an old story. A student asked his spiritual teacher to best describe enlightenment so the student would know when and if he experienced it. The master replied, *"Enlightenment is drinking when you're thirsty and eating when you're hungry."* Then certainly enlightenment is listening to our body's feedback and responding correctly to it. So we could add, **if you are tired, take a break!**

I realize that this thought is almost anti-American. In fact, this is the only country in the world that doesn't take a break in the afternoon. In my travels around the world, I find that everyone takes afternoon breaks, in some countries for hours. In California many people ask me if I have any tonics for energy. When I ask why, they reply that they have an energy slump in the mid-afternoon shortly after lunch.

I tell them that this is normal and to take a brief nap. This is what the rest of the world does, but we think this is outrageous. The typical response is to have a cup of coffee, beat up our adrenal glands and blast ourselves back to consciousness.

I strongly urge that you take a few days off work and focus on your aggressive purification. Just turn a two-day weekend into a four-day one. Work can live without you for two days. If you don't, it is likely that your cold will drag on and you will be in pain, feel like crap, and suffer for weeks instead of hours, and will probably get another cold or infection again soon. It's your choice, two days off work or 2 to 3 weeks in bed.

When contemplating about life on the death bed, not one of my patients ever told me that they wished they spent more time at the office. So come on, lighten up. Go home and have a fun time setting up the best natural healing environment you can. But don't wimp out, and remember, if I was at your house–well, just visualize two things: my foot and your ass.

Since it is a normal function of the body to have a purification now and then, this is great. Don't think of yourself as sick; think of your body as cleansing. Remember, whenever the body does a repair job it always does it 150%. In other words, when your body defends itself from an infection, especially if assisted and not drugged, it will also use this time to do some extra house cleaning, to burn up and eliminate accumulated toxins and poisons. Your body will use this time to eat up and destroy all sorts of things that you didn't even know you had. Even the beginnings of diseases that would've surfaced years from now will be destroyed.

This should be a time for meditation, moderate movement and pure rest.

Step 5: Attitude Program

Get rid of all your negative thoughts about colds, influenza and fevers and begin new positive thoughts and affirmations about your body healing itself and doing a routine self-cleanse. Have fun and enjoy your new aggressive purification routines and make this a fun experience. Since your body has decided to do a detoxification program, assist it by giving it the best program you can.

Tell 20 jokes every day, laugh, tell someone you love them, especially yourself, and remember to open that window and get some fresh air. It will lift your spirits and supply you with disease-fighting oxygen.

❝ *Your Immune System is LISTENING to and REACTING to your emotional dialogue.* **❞**
— *Dr. Schulze*

Step 6: Just say no to drugs

NEVER, NEVER, NEVER take any drugs, over-the-counter, under-the-counter, behind-the-counter, especially ones that suppress symptoms or reduce fevers. All of these drugs go directly AGAINST what your body is trying to do – to heal you – and this can be very dangerous. It can even kill you.

NEVER, NEVER, NEVER reduce a fever with drugs. Many people have died not from fevers, but trying to suppress them.

By drinking lots of liquids and keeping hydrated a fever will never, ever hurt you.

A fever is part of your body's immune response. It is called leukotaxis and this function PROTECTS you. For every degree of temperature rise in your body the speed at which your white blood cells (your immune cells) can travel to the infection and kill and eat up the bad bacteria and virus IS DOUBLED. This means if you are running a temperature of 104 degrees your white blood cells can reach the infection 64 TIMES FASTER THAN NORMAL. Now I ask you, why, when your body is creating a fever to speed up your immune system to fight off, kill and eat harmful bacteria and viruses, would you want to slow that process down? That would be insane. Modern medicine is trying so hard to make you comfortable and pain-free they are willing to go against your body, against healing, if necessary.

Fevers are never dangerous as long as you **keep hydrated** and don't continue to poison the body. Never use any drugs that suppress fevers, coughs, runny noses, or any of the symptoms of colds and flu. If you do, you cripple your immune system and block your body's natural ability to kill off colds and flu.

Dr. Schulze's other powerful herbal formulae
TO STOP COLDS & FLU

THROAT & TONSIL

A Specific Herbal Tonic for Sore Throats and Swollen Glands.

This formula is to be used as a gargle and is specific for sore throats and inflamed or infected throats, tonsils, and adenoids. Often this is one of the first signs of a cold or flu. This numbing formula greatly relieves the pain of a sore throat, but also kills bacteria, viruses, fungi and is antiseptic. It stimulates a local immune response and the thick consistency makes it adhere to your throat and tonsils. This formula puts the fire out.

Botanical Ingredients

Echinacea angustifolia root, Fresh Garlic bulb, Habanero pepper, Peppermint leaf and Peppermint essential oil in a base of California Fig concentrate.

Throat & Tonsil Dosage

Use 1 - 4 droppersful squirted directly onto tonsils and throat. Gargle for at least 1 full minute and swallow. Repeat as often as necessary.

LUNG FORMULA

A Specific Herbal Formula for Clearing, Drying Up and Disinfecting the Sinus Passages and the Lungs.

My Lung Formula works in two main ways. First, the plant chemicals in this tonic will dilate your bronchial tubes, forcing them to open wider so you can breathe easier. Second, while most doctors prescribe drugs to stop you from coughing, I have added herbs to this tonic that actually promote coughing. That's because you need to get the mucous out of your lungs or you can literally drown. Plus, if you suppress your cough it'll just make the whole miserable experience last longer. In a nutshell, my Lung Formula makes it easier to breathe as well as cough up and out mucous.

Botanical Ingredients

Lobelia leaf and seed, Elecampane root, Coltsfoot leaf, Horehound leaf, Licorice root, Kola nut, Coffee bean, Cherry bark, Thyme leaf, Fennel seed, Peppermint leaf and essential oil.

Lung Formula Dosage

Take 30 to 60 drops in 2 ounces of water 2 to 4 times daily.

AIR DETOX

This formula disinfects the air and helps you to BREATHE EASIER.

My Air Detox destroys germs in the air. It's a great disinfectant for the bedroom, sick room, bathroom, even the office. It keeps germs from spreading to the whole family.

This is the exact formula I made to disinfect my clinic. With many very sick patients, some literally crawling into the door, my clinic smelled horrible and the air was literally thick with germs. I needed to develop a formula that would make the place smell good, and only pure, undiluted essential oils are strong enough to do that. But I also needed it to disinfect the air of my clinic, to kill the bacteria, viruses, fungi and God knows what else was lurking in the air, especially in the bathroom. At home, not only does this formula disinfect the air in your house and stop the spreading of colds and flu, it is essential for high-risk households with children, pregnant women and senior citizens. This is a very strong formula, so strong it can stain, melt plastic and we have to ship it with two sprayers because it often eats up and dissolves the first sprayer when you are only half-finished with the bottle. This formula not only kills EVERYTHING in the air, but is really nice sprayed onto your pillow at night to kill germs and help you breathe easier all night long. Use an old pillow case because it will stain. In fact, all of my herbal products will stain, because there is actually something **in** them.

Botanical Ingredients

100% essential oils of eucalyptus, lime, lemon, orange and grapefruit.

Air Detox Dosage

Spray as often as you like. Keep a bottle in every bathroom in the house.

DEEP TISSUE OIL

This formula can take the PAIN of an infection away and let you sleep!

I could tell you a hundred uses for just colds and flu, that is one of the reasons my patients named this formula a "miracle in a bottle." You can rub it on your chest at night. The vapors will decongest your sinus and lungs. Dilute it with a little olive oil if doing this on children. You can rub it on your neck to relieve the pain of swollen glands and it will increase the lymphatic circulation. During fevers often your bones and lower back can ache; Deep Tissue Oil will take the pain away and increase the circulation. For sore throats you can take a few droppersful in your mouth and let them drip down your throat. You can even carefully squirt a dropperful right on a swollen infected tonsil. If you have sinus pain and pressure, rub it anywhere on the head, temples, bridge of the nose, even up inside the mouth on the soft palate. Are you getting the idea yet? You are only limited by your imagination. This formula is especially great when you are sick and wake up in pain and can't get back to sleep. Rub it on the painful areas, and in a few minutes you will be back in dreamland.

Botanical Ingredients

Wintergreen oil, Peppermint oil concentrate, Cayenne peppers, Ginger root, Arnica flowers, Saint John's wort flowers, Marigold (Calendula) flowers, and organic virgin olive oil.

Deep Tissue Oil Dosage

CAUTION, THIS FORMULA IS VERY STRONG.
Do not get it in your eyes, ears, penis, vagina, anus (at least by accident). Just put a few drops to a dropperful in the palm of your hand, and with a finger apply to the area desired.

Real People. Real Results.

"Dear Dr. Schulze,

I am writing to tell you that I think your products are wonderful!!
As for Deep Tissue Oil, I have gone to bed with my neck so stiff
I could barely turn my head without hurting, and with the oil
rubbed in my neck and shoulders, the next morning my neck
was completely, and I mean completely back to normal. To
loosely paraphrase Will Rogers, I never met one of your
products that I didn't like!"
— K.B. Stone Mountain, GA

"I strongly urged all my patients and students to keep all of these formulae on hand during the winter months. The speed in which you use these formulae at the onset of an infection is what greatly determines the length and severity of a cold or flu."

CHAPTER FIVE
WHO IS DR. SCHULZE?

PERSONAL HEALING

When Dr. Schulze was only 11 years old, his father suffered a massive heart attack and died. Three years later, when he was 14, his mother also died of a heart attack. Both were only 55 years old when they died.

At the age of 16, after a year of ill health, Dr. Schulze was diagnosed by medical doctors with a genetic heart deformity and deformed heart valves. The doctors told him that unless he underwent open heart surgery, his weak and deformed heart wouldn't be able to supply sufficient blood to an adult body and he would be dead by the age of 20.

He declined to have the surgery and instead made it his mission to discover alternative ways to heal his heart. After three years of intensive self-immersion in natural healing programs and herbal formulae, he was given a clean bill of health by the same medical doctors who had told him he would die without surgery. His heart was healed. After curing himself of this so-called "incurable" disease, he set out on a mission to help others and enrolled himself into Naturopathic & Herbal College.

EDUCATION AND CREDENTIALS

Dr. Schulze studied with the famous European Naturopath, Paavo Airola. He trained under, and then served an internship with, the famous natural healer Dr. Bernard Jensen. He also studied and apprenticed with "America's greatest herbalist," the late, great Dr. John Christopher, graduating to teach alongside him until his death. Besides having a doctorate in Herbology, a doctorate in Natural Medicine and three degrees in Iridology, he is certified in eight different styles of Body Therapy and holds three black belts in the martial arts.

CLINICAL EXPERIENCE

In the early 1970's he opened his first natural healing clinic in New York, and then later moved his clinic to Southern California. He operated his natural healing clinic in America for almost twenty years. During this same time he also managed and directed other natural healing clinics in Europe and Asia. In his two decades of practice, he treated thousands of patients, and in the second of those two decades he became famous for his intensive natural healing programs and his powerful herbal formulae.

Dr. Schulze's natural therapy programs and herbal formulae are now used in clinics all over the world and have assisted countless numbers of people to create healing miracles and regain their health. He is considered an innovator, a purist, even an extremist by many of his colleagues, but to his patients he was considered a lifesaver.

Dr. Schulze dared to pioneer new techniques and therapies which went far beyond what most people thought possible with alternative medicine. The outcome of his work has been the achievement of miraculous and unprecedented results. His herbal formulae and natural healing programs are used in clinics worldwide to help people heal themselves of any number of supposedly incurable diseases. The positive results have reverberated throughout both the natural and medical communities.

A PASSIONATE, ELECTRIFYING TEACHER

After Dr. Christopher's death, Dr. Schulze continued to teach at his school for over twelve years. He has served as the Director of the College of Herbology and Natural Healing in the United Kingdom for eleven years and is also Co-Director of The Osho School for Naturopathic Medicine in England, France, and Spain. He has taught and lectured at numerous universities, including Cambridge and Oxford Universities in England, Trinity Medical College in Ireland, Omega Institute in New York, Cortijo Romero in Spain, and other natural therapy and herbal institutes worldwide. He has been the guest speaker at numerous churches and also on numerous radio and television shows. He is loved for his intensity, passion, sense of humor, creativity, and his exciting, enthusiastic, and evangelical style of teaching. He is mostly recognized for his unequaled understanding of natural healing.

AMERICAN BOTANICAL PHARMACY

Dr. Schulze continues his healing mission today through his daily work to reveal the truth about the unlimited healing power of our bodies. After fifteen years of manufacturing his own herbal formulations in his clinic, Dr. Schulze opened the American Botanical Pharmacy, the sole distributor of his industrial-strength, pharmaceutical grade extracts, in 1994.

Dr. Schulze is also a leader in exposing fraud in medical, pharmaceutical and even herbal industries. To this day he continues to promote the message of natural healing through his videos, audios, books, and newsletters.

CHAPTER SIX: HOW TO ORDER

NOW THAT YOU'VE READ ABOUT IT,
DO SOMETHING ABOUT IT.

INTERESTED IN DR. SCHULZE'S POWERFUL HERBAL FORMULAE?

to order PRODUCTS or request a FREE Catalog AND AUDIO TAPE

Call: 1-800-HERB-DOC (437-2362) • Visit: www.herbdoc.com

Dr. Schulze's Famous

COLD & FLU
TREATMENT PROGRAM

Treating Colds and Influenza begins with my new Cold & Flu Program. PERIOD. Antibiotics are useless for influenza even though patients demand them, and flu shots are, pure and simple, an ineffective gamble with YOUR health! Strengthening your body's natural ability to fight against viruses is your FIRST STEP in getting the upper hand against Colds and Influenza this season.

✔ **Start this program at the first sign of symptoms!**

✔ **Antibiotics are useless against any viruses!**

✔ **Stop a cold or flu dead in its tracks!**

Cold & Flu Program: Includes: 2 Echinacea Plus, 1 SuperTonic, 1 Air Detox (2 oz.), 2 Cold & Flu Detox Teas, 2 Cold and Flu Detox Bath Packs, 1 "25 Ways to Prevent and Treat Colds & Flu" Book, 1 Quick Start Directions

INTERESTED IN DR. SCHULZE'S POWERFUL HERBAL FORMULAE?

to order PRODUCTS or request a FREE Catalog AND AUDIO TAPE

Call: 1-800-HERB-DOC (437-2362) • Visit: www.herbdoc.com

MORE NATURAL HEALING RESOURCES
FROM DR. SCHULZE

Ask about ALL Dr. Schulze's Natural Healing Books, DVD/Videos and Audio Tapes

3 MUST-READ BOOKS IN THIS SERIES!

- **HEALING COLON DISEASE NATURALLY**

- **HEALING LIVER DISEASE NATURALLY**

- **HEALING KIDNEY DISEASE NATURALLY**

Now Only $7.00

TO ORDER PRODUCTS OR REQUEST A FREE CATALOG AND AUDIO TAPE
CALL 1-877-TEACH ME (832-2463)

INTERESTED IN DR. SCHULZE'S POWERFUL HERBAL FORMULAE?

TO ORDER PRODUCTS OR REQUEST
A FREE CATALOG AND AUDIO TAPE

Call: 1-800-HERB-DOC (437-2362)
Visit: www.herbdoc.com

Available Exclusively from American Botanical Pharmacy

"The main metabolic function of your IMMUNE SYSTEM, and your BODY, is to constantly HEAL and REPAIR itself; REPAIR you."

– Dr. Richard Schulze

"Your Immune System is LISTENING to and REACTING to your emotional dialogue."

– Dr. Richard Schulze